I0487432

100 *Tools* & *Resources*
To *Boost* your *Brand*

Written by
Yerodin Ghedi Adwin Beluchi

Editor: JNF Enterprises

Cover Illustrator: Jordan Nichols

Publisher:
Black History Enterprises
Houston, TX, 77057
Email: admin@blackhistoryent.net

ISBN: 978-0-578-23721-3

Printed in the United States of America

Contents

Dedication

This book is dedicated to my brothers and sisters in the struggle of trying to start and operate their own businesses without any significant prior knowledge or training on how to become a successful entrepreneur.

Acknowledgments

My mother, Gwendolyn Thomas Nichols, who has been a big part of the reason why I've made it this far through all of the mental and emotional challenges I've faced, because she's been supporting me from day one and any time I started to feel like nobody truly cared about me, she was there to check on my well-being. My father, Richard Nichols, who was the first person I had ever seen work for himself when I was only about 4 years old, who also schooled me on his trade of concrete finishing and instilled in me a sense of hard work up through my young adulthood years.

Preface

Knowledge is power, and this book is perfect for the reference library for any professional and business owner who is committed to growth. This book includes a long list of tools and resources to boost your brand, but it also gives you a breakdown as to why and how to utilize each one. One of the toughest challenges to starting and maintaining a business is access to information about various resources that will assist you in operating every aspect of your business. From the initial registration of your business to the marketing of your brand and hiring of your employees, this book is loaded with valuable tools and resources to give you the edge you need to be successful as a business owner.

Preech's inspiration for writing this book came from considering how many so-called African and African-American entrepreneurs, like himself, are not presented with such an array of tools and resources, because most of us did not come from a family of entrepreneurs or successful business executives. Unfortunately, most of us come from families that only know how to teach us how to work and not create. It was only after I realized that I cannot place my career into anyone's hands but my own that I got busy creating, speaking, thinking and researching, I had to go up the learning curve quickly, and sometimes I did not know what I did not know. As an entrepreneur, in the era of Coronavirus, being able to have tools to drive revenue online is critical.

Preech is an entrepreneur that I met a few years ago, and watched him grow Entrepreneurs of Color Magazine, share his business wisdom, and engage in the small business community. I applaud him for putting together this resource for small business owners. If you are just starting out in the world of business this is a great resource for you to consider adding to your library. Do not just allow this book to collect dust. Research the platforms shared. Ask yourself questions and leverage your tools to discover answers. Just like a plumber or carpenter, every entrepreneur needs the best tools to pursue success.

This book is a great resource for anyone who is interested in going into business or identifying ways to increase revenue of their current business or employer. This book is also a great resource for individuals who work in the fields of marketing, branding, business development, advertising, public relations and human resources.

Zhe L. Scott

Foreword

"Success is to be measured not so much by the position one reaches in life but by the obstacles one overcomes." - Booker Taliaferro Washington

We elevate our life by transitioning between realms of purpose, commerce, and profits. Our ultimate goal as entrepreneurs is to achieve a posture of undeniable influence, impact, and intentional action with every system, process, and result we apply our hands to produce. Our interpersonal peace will align us with our birthright, by any means necessary, as we face everything and rise higher to be a force in global marketplaces. There are times when life presents an outpouring of opportunities yet only when our mindset (faith) aligns with our purpose (execution) while hiring talented entities (economics) to meet, to supply, to fund, to support, to distribute, to purchase, to consume, to utilize, to review, to recommend, to purchase again, and to ultimately - propel a brand's recognition for current and future generations to experience.

Preech has and is operating in a space of excellence by remaining true in the skillsets he has mastered from various trials and tribulations while learning the crafts of Branding, Marketing, and Networking. His resume has scaled the networth of many brands worldwide. It is not by chance every brand who follows the wisdom shared by Preech have discovered substantial results in their digital fingerprint, their automatic sales transactions, their clear connection with ideal tribes, and their overall Brand-image.

LaToya Rose, M.ED, AFSP

Introduction

These days, especially considering the global pandemic we're experiencing here in 2020, it is imperative as an entrepreneur or business owner that you are informed on various ways to operate your business. Otherwise, you may find yourself having to close your business due to not being able to adapt. Even before COVID-19 was a household term, being able to "pivot", as many in business put it; was essential to being able to survive as a business owner. For example, when social media became an everyday way of life for people to communicate and find news, entrepreneurs and companies of all sizes had to adapt by creating and building a social media presence. The term "Social Media Manager" has even become a job title that strictly requires someone to be well-versed in what is now known as social media marketing.

Going back even further, the introduction of the worldwide web otherwise known as the internet changed the way people present and market their businesses, because people began to use it as a main source for finding businesses of interest. In addition, once Google had established itself as the most used search engine, businesses with websites had to adapt to learning ways to get good placement in Google's Search Engine results. Introducing a term now known as SEO or *"Search Engine Optimization."* Even before the internet was a thing, going back to the pioneering times of radio and television, businesses had to learn how to effectively market themselves on the various radio & TV platforms, as it had become a way most people were looking for businesses of interest.

Let's take a look at Blockbuster for example. Blockbuster was once a very popular way for people to rent and purchase movies and video games. But, after the internet had become something almost everyone was using and because Blockbuster didn't adapt by creating and building an internet presence, they were forced to go out of business, closing down all of their stores worldwide. Another example is RadioShack. In February 2015, Radio Shack filed for Chapter 11 bankruptcy protection. RadioShack failed to adapt and stay relevant when most electronics sales shifted online, and the retailer was stuck in brick-and-mortar locations only. Another great example of how a business failed to adapt to change is Nokia. In the late 1990s & early 2000s, Nokia was the global leader in mobile phones. However, when the internet became more popular, other mobile companies started understanding how data, not voice, was the future of communication. Nokia failed to switch their focus to software and kept focusing on hardware because management feared alienating current users, if they changed too much.

You don't want to be that business owner who feared change and eventually had to discontinue business operations or even worse...file bankruptcy. I employ you to take charge of the survival of your business and relevancy of your brand by making sure you stay up to date with ever changing trends in the business world. It's one thing to still be in business, but it's another thing to actually thrive and stay in business. If you've gone so far as to purchase this book, then I applaud you for being serious about the future of your brand.

Chapter 1

Social Media Marketing

Because it is one of the most utilized ways to market a brand, in this first chapter, I'm going to share with you some tools and resources regarding social media marketing. Many of them, I'm sure you've already heard about, but instead of just giving you a list, I'm also going to go over some tips on how to best utilize social media for your brand. So, even if you're already familiar with some of the resources on this list, you may want to consider my coaching advice on how to get the most out of them and adjust your strategy for how you utilize them.

1. Facebook

What was once a network for college students has grown into a communication medium for people of all ages around the world, furthermore, it's grown into the most utilized way to market a business for free. But, here's the problem with that...now that Facebook has become the large platform that it is, its algorithm for how to reach people has become dependent on two things. How much people like you and how much money you spend. If you're not what many call a "social influencer", you could spend all day making posts on

Facebook and still not reach a substantial amount of people and the time it takes to become an influencer could take years. So, if you're not already someone who people can't wait to see post again, your chances of getting anywhere with Facebook are cut by a large margin. Then you have those people who spend all day copying & pasting their campaigns and sending it to random people's inboxes. As someone who will quickly ignore such an effort, if I don't already know much about you, I can almost guarantee you that this will cause you to waste a great deal of valuable time.

Now, let's talk about paid advertising. I'm sure many of you reading this have at least seen an ad on Facebook, if you haven't already actually posted one yourself. Maybe you've seen results or maybe you haven't. The thing to keep in mind about advertising on any social media platform is that you're competing with much larger companies who have much bigger marketing budgets than the average entrepreneur or small business. With that being said, if you're not allotting a substantial amount of money for your daily budget, then chances are, your ad will get pushed to the bottom of the priority list and your investment will essentially go to waste. In any form of advertising, the bottom line goal is to get as many impressions as possible. Impressions are basically the number of times your ad is seen. A good minimum budget to consider for social media advertising is $10/day.

2. Instagram

Once its own independent company, Instagram is now owned by Facebook, Inc. Which means that when utilizing it, you have to consider some of the same things you have to consider with Facebook. So, just like Facebook's algorithm is more friendly to influencers and those who pay for advertising, Instagram is the same way.

Now, let's talk about some methods for utilizing Instagram. One of the things that separates Instagram from Facebook is what we know as hashtags. I'm assuming that if you're reading this book, by now you know what hashtags are. But, the question is how well are you utilizing them? As of now, Instagram only allows up to 30 hashtags for your post. Which may sound like a lot, but when you consider the many variations of hashtags that can be used and depending on your business model, you may actually have to omit some of them that come to mind when making a post. Of course, you could always just come up with your own, but it would also suit you to do some research on which ones are mostly used. Another thing to consider is the order of your hashtags by putting the most used ones first. Because Instagram only allows you to post images and videos, you will have to be creative about how to post text on images, which I will discuss further in this book.

3. Twitter

Although Twitter may not necessarily be as popular as Facebook and Instagram are, it is still a great way to spread awareness about your brand. One thing that separates Twitter from other social networks is that information circulates faster on its platform. You can actually scroll through Twitter's Timeline and witness different conversational threads displayed as individual tweets. Which essentially makes you a spectator to what everyone else is talking about. Whereas on other platforms like Facebook and Instagram, you actually have to click to show the full thread of comments on a single post. This makes Twitter one of the most effective ways to spread news and just like Instagram, Twitter is dominated by hashtags, whereas you can even see what's trending in your area, which virtually increases just how fast information spreads on its platform.

4. LinkedIn

You may have heard of LinkedIn or have even created an account, but have yet to actually utilize it. If you're not already using LinkedIn, you may want to consider signing up. The thing that separates LinkedIn from other social media platforms is its professional environment. LinkedIn is mostly used by college students, college graduates, business executives and business owners. Which essentially makes it potentially a much more profitable platform for marketing your brand, because the average income of its users are arguably much higher than that of other social media networks. In addition, LinkedIn users are more likely to engage with your posts after you've established yourself, as it is a place where people are actively searching for valuable information opposed to just laughs and giggles. I've actually seen posts reach reactions and interactions in the thousands for influential people. Something I've never seen on any other platform without it being a paid ad.

Social Media Management

In addition to social media networks, there are also platforms for managing your accounts. These platforms make everyday management of social media marketing less time consuming. If you are someone who plans to utilize more than one social media account, you may want to consider taking advantage of one or more of these platforms. Some of them offer free services, whereas others require a payment. Many of them even offer analytics to give you insight on how well your accounts are doing. The biggest advantage of utilizing a social media management platform is being able to schedule multiple posts ahead of time, so that you can dedicate more of your time to focusing on other aspects of your business.

5. Later

I first learned about Later in 2017 after obtaining a new client for my social media marketing services who required me to use it if she was going to utilize my services. At the time though, I was already utilizing other similar platforms to manage my social media networks. To be honest, my first impression of it wasn't a good one, because the platforms I was using at the time allowed me to schedule posts that would go out automatically, whereas Later required you to respond to a notification at the scheduled time of your post which basically served as a reminder to make the post yourself. I found that to actually defeat the purpose of utilizing it as a social media management platform. However, I recently signed up for Later with a free account just to see what changes were made. Thankfully, it now gives you the option to automatically post to your accounts. Another cool aspect of Later is that it offers analytics to track your follower growth, post impressions, profile views and website clicks. If you're someone who wants to utilize a free option for social media management to just free up some of your time until it's something that you will take more advantage of later, then you should consider looking into Later.

Learn more at Later.com

6. OnlyPult

Upon initially signing up for and utilizing OnlyPult, I can honestly say that I fell in love with it. That was back in 2017 and since then updates have been implemented making it an even more valuable tool for social media management. OnlyPult is set up for you to give access to up to 5 Social Media Managers, so that they don't have to have access to your actual account. If you're someone who plans to hire a SMM, then you may want to consider this option. OnlyPult is the only platform I know that allows you to manage so many different social media networks including Facebook, Instagram, Twitter, LinkedIn, Google My Business, YouTube, TikTok, Tumblr, WordPress, Telegram, VKontakte & Odnoklassniki, allowing management of up to 40 different accounts. It even gives you a breakdown of when your followers mostly interact with your posts, so that you can be more aware of the days and times to actually make a post to maximize results.

Learn more at onlypult.com

7. Hootsuite

Hootsuite was actually the first social media management platform I had ever heard of. I believe it was in 2012 when a business partner first introduced me to it. What makes Hootsuite stand out from other social media management platforms is that it allows you to manage your inbox and create what are known as "streams", which gives you a chance to filter the view of your social media accounts. Hootsuite even has what they call "Hootsuite Academy", where they offer training and certifications. If you're someone with more than one brand, which means you probably have people assigned as "Teams" to those different brands based on their expertise then Hootsuite is a great option for you, because you can easily give team members access to networks for specific brands.

Learn more at hootsuite.com

8. Social Hackettes

Social Hackettes is a very popular black-owned Social Media Management company founded in 2014 and based in Orange, NJ that offers management for many different social media platforms including Facebook, Instagram, Twitter, YouTube, LinkedIn, TikTok and more. I've come across quite a few social media management solutions, but not one that offers management for so many different platforms. They also offer Website Development and Search Engine Optimization Services. If you would like to utilize an array of social media outlets without the hassle of maintaining all of them on your own and/or you want website development and social media marketing offered as a combined service, consider checking out Social Hackettes as your solution.

Learn more at socialhackettes.com

Chapter 2

Domain & Web Hosting

Earlier in this book, I mentioned how the rise in the popularity of the internet forced businesses to create and maintain a web presence. So, I would hope by now that you see the importance of having a website, if you don't already have one. No matter what your business model is, having a website will undoubtedly increase your chances of attracting customers. So, in this chapter, I'm going to share with you some different options to consider for domain and web hosting. Depending on your business model, you will need to take into consideration which web hosting option is best suited for your brand. Some of these options cater more to those with a focus on blogging, whereas others cater more to those with a focus on eCommerce. Of course, there are some that have a rather balanced focus on both aspects.

9. GoDaddy

GoDaddy is the most popular Domain Registrar out there right now, which you've probably already heard about, even if you've never used it. One thing I will personally say makes GoDaddy stand out is that they have exceptional customer service. Their lines are open all day every day. They even offer free website hosting. GoDaddy even offers integration with popular brands such as WordPress & Office 365. Don't have a professional email with your own domain name yet? GoDaddy has an option for that too. They also offer a web design service for people who wish to hire a professional web designer.

Learn more at GoDaddy.com

10. Wix

What was once an option not very many businesses were utilizing, by constantly implementing updates, Wix has become one of the more popular web hosting services. I, myself, even use it to publish my site. What I like most about it, is that it gives you nearly full control over designing your website from scratch, inch by inch, without any need for a background in HTML. Giving beginners of website design the ability to create professional looking websites. However, keep in mind that creating something from scratch that's appealing to others may require a great deal of your time, so if you're not someone looking to dedicate a lot of time to designing a website, you may want to utilize another platform or hire a professional, which Wix has a service for. Its eCommerce options integrate with a number of different popular payment processing platforms, which I will mention later in this book. Wix is loaded with many different plug-ins and add-ons, such as social media feeds and pop-ups that will enhance the overall look and feel of your website. If you don't mind having a subdomain, you can even publish websites for free. Wix also offers domain registration, custom email domains and email marketing campaigns. If you don't mind dedicating a lot of time to designing a website and you want the power of completely customizable features, then Wix would be a great option for you.

Learn more at Wix.com

11. WordPress

One of the most popular web hosting platforms that has been around for a long time, WordPress is a great option for building a website. While collaborating with a business partner a few years ago, I was given the opportunity to view the backend of building a site with WordPress. I can definitely see why so many people use it. It simplifies the process of creating a website by giving you access to many different themes, so that you can spend more time on things like sales and blogging. If you're someone who plans to put a great deal of time into blogging on your site, I'd definitely recommend Wordpress. Just like Wix, Wordpress is suited with thousands of add-ons to enhance the look and feel of your website. Wordpress websites also have excellent loading times due to the simplicity of designing on its platform. It even allows you to create subdomains, so if you're looking to create a social media network of your own, without the need for your own servers, this could be a great option for you. I, myself have even considered moving my website to WordPress, but after spending so much time building my site on Wix, I haven't been in too much of a hurry to do so.

Learn more at wordpress.com

12. Shopify

Focused primarily on the eCommerce aspect of a website, Shopify has grown into one of the most popular ways, if not the most popular way, to build an online store. One of the things that stands out most to me about Shopify, is its integration with Instagram. Businesses can create an online store within the Instagram app itself, making it really easy for people to shop with you without having to actually go to your website. With 24/7 customer support, Shopify is a great option to consider when looking for a web hosting solution. If you're someone who plans to offer a wide range of products, you should definitely consider Shopify as your website host.

Learn more at shopify.com

13. Blogger and Domains by Google

In addition to the many other business solutions that Google provides, they've also added domain registration. Now, I can't say that I've registered a domain with Google, but I wouldn't doubt that doing so gives you an edge when it comes to placement in Google's Search Engine Optimization. Google even offers a website building platform, which many know as "Blogger." I've actually built a website on Blogger about 8 years or so ago and even though it wasn't as all-inclusive as other options, it was definitely easy to do. It even has an incorporated social media community to it, where you can connect with other bloggers. Given the name, Blogger, it's a great option for anyone planning to do a lot of blogging. Especially if you want your articles to get good placement on Google Search pages. You can even post to Blogger directly from Google Docs.

Learn more at domains.google.com

14. Weebly

Now integrated with Square Payment Processing, Weebly has become another popular web hosting platform. Now, I haven't personally used Weebly to create a website before, but from the looks of it, it offers tons of themes for building the overall look and feel of your website. So, if you're someone who wants to simplify the process of building a website and you prefer Square as a payment processor, then Weebly may be the option for you. Similar to Wix, Weebly has a drop-and-drop feature that allows you to select add-ons and put them in a specific place on your website giving you more power to customize how your site looks. Boasting that over 50 million people already use Weebly, I definitely don't doubt it as a viable option for web hosting.
Learn more at weebly.com

15. Square eCommerce

Now a competitor for Shopify, Square now offers an option for businesses to create a website strictly focused on making sales. They even offer this service for free. The only time you pay for utilizing it is when you actually make a sale, whereas they take out a percentage and a fee of your transactions. It even functions with Apple Pay & Google Pay. Just like Shopify, Square also integrates with Instagram. Its features even accommodate for businesses that offer delivery and pick up options. As this is a fairly new option for web hosting and considering the already high level of popularity that Square has as a payment processor, you can bet that this one will continue to grow.

Learn more at squareup.com

16. Yola

This one is rather new to me, but after taking the time to research it, I can see why it has become so popular, having been featured in numerous business magazines such as Forbes and The Wall Street Journal. For one, it's free for up to 2 websites. The catch to this is that you can only have up to 2 pages per website. The other catch to this is that you will have to stick with a subdomain, making your site less brandable. In addition to the free option, they have a paid subscription which includes domain registration and management, custom email accounts, an online store and more.
If you just want a couple of easy to design landing pages for free just to at least have an online presence outside of social media or you want to be able to manage most of your online tools and resources in one place, then Yola might be the option for you.

Learn more at Yola.com

17. Tumblr

Built with the blogger in mind, Tumblr not only allows you to create a blog site for free, but just like Blogger, it also incorporates a social media aspect to it, making it stand out as a way to blog. Like other social media platforms, people can share or "reblog" your Tumblr posts to their blog. Creating my first blog site with Tumblr in 2010, I eventually fell in love with the platform and at one point advocated it as the best social media community out there. My magazine, *Entrepreneurs of Color Magazine* even had its first online presence outside of social media on Tumblr. Have more than one blog idea in mind? Tumblr allows you to create multiple blogs that can easily be managed within its platform. Unlike other web hosting platforms, Tumblr allows you to connect a custom domain free of charge. If you're someone who strictly wants to blog and generate revenue or brand awareness in that way, while interacting with a large community of people, then Tumblr is definitely a great option for you.

Learn more at Tumblr.com

18. Whois

Now, this one is new to me. After taking the time to research it, I can see that it's probably one of the cheapest, if not the cheapest domain registration, email hosting & website hosting solutions out there. But, that doesn't mean it's not useful. One thing that stands out most to me is that you never lose ownership of your domains. It was actually suggested to me after expressing how a domain which I put a great deal of work into popularizing had been purchased by someone else after I went more than a year with no business activity. I'm actually thinking about switching over after my terms are up with GoDaddy. However, I can see that GoDaddy has much better customer service options. But, if you're someone who feels like you'll almost never need customer service or you're willing to settle with email support and you're on a budget, then this could be a great option for you.

Learn more at whois.com

Chapter 3

Accounting & Payment Processing

Nowadays most transactions are handled online and/or with debit or credit cards. So, if you're that business owner still depending strictly on cash transactions, you're definitely missing out on a great deal of income opportunities. In fact, it's probably safe to say that more than 50% of transactions these days are done with a debit or credit card. Credit and debit card transactions make it easier to do accounting. But, depending on your sales volume and your knowledge of taxation, you may need to actually hire an Accountant. So, with that being said, in this chapter, I'm going to present to you a list of options for accounting and payment processing.

19. PayPal

A pioneer to the online payment processing industry, PayPal may not be as popular as it once was, but it is still a great option to have for accepting payments. My favorite aspect of PayPal is its ability to set up recurring payments and accept donations. There is a Subscribe and a Donate button for PayPal that you can integrate by HTML into any website. Essentially, it is the integratable buttons that makes PayPal stand out from other payment processing companies. PayPal also provides you with a personal PayPal.me link that you can send other PayPal users to easily send you money. Like many other payment processing companies, PayPal allows you to send invoices, track accounting and order a debit card to easily access the money in your account. You can even set up invoices to allow customers and clients to make a minimum deposit instead of having to pay it all at once. Almost everywhere you shop offers PayPal as an option for making secure payments. The only downside to utilizing PayPal as a payment processing solution is that outside of invoicing, your customers and clients will need to have PayPal accounts setup.

Learn more at paypal.com

20. Square

Since its inception, Square has become one of the most popular ways, if not the most popular way, to process business transactions. Unlike many other payment processing companies, Square offers a card reader to swipe debit and credit card payments without requiring you to meet a minimum monthly revenue. Square now even gives you a debit card to easily access the money in your account. Square is an integratable option for accepting payments that most web hosting companies offer. The most popular component of Square that a lot of people use is CashApp. CashApp has it to where you can easily send and request money by a phone number or user ID proceeded by a dollar sign such as $blackhistoryent. CashApp even gives you a debit card and an account and routing number to use for direct deposits. I, myself, have used CashApp a number of times as a way for people without cash to pay for entry into an event. As for apps that offer a money transfer service, CashApp is definitely the most popular. Even if you have another preferred way of accepting payments, I would suggest that you include CashApp as an option for customers and clients.

Learn more at squareup.com

21. Venmo

Owned by PayPal, Venmo is slowly making its way to becoming one of the most popular ways to send and receive money. Just like PayPal and Square, Venmo offers a free debit card to easily access the money in your account. I actually just started using Venmo as a payment method and I'm glad I've included it as an option, because oftentimes it's how people ask me to pay for a product or service. Although Venmo doesn't come with as many features as PayPal and Square does, it's still a good alternative for accepting payments that you may want to consider offering. In my opinion, you can never have too many ways to accept payments.

Learn more at venmo.com

22. Zelle

Zelle is rather new to me. But, just like Venmo, it's slowly becoming one of the most popular ways to send and receive money. There are even many banks that have Zelle integrated into their mobile apps, whereas people can send money directly to your bank account with a phone number or email address. Zelle is actually owned by Bank of America, BB&T, Capital One, JPMorgan Chase, PNC Bank, US Bank and Wells Fargo. Just like Venmo, Zelle is limited to what features it offers, because it wasn't necessarily designed for businesses. Nevertheless it's also still a good alternative for accepting payments that you may want to consider offering.

Learn more at zellepay.com

23. Stripe

Stripe isn't as popular as other payment processing solutions, but it could still be beneficial to utilize as a way to collect payments. Mainly because Stripe allows you to collect recurring payments. Stripe even has a way for you to offer promotional rates and trial periods. There are also web hosting services that allow integration with Stripe, so you can collect payments right from your website. So, if you have a business that offers subscriptions, sponsorships and/or memberships and relays on a daily, weekly, monthly and/or yearly payments, then Stripe is definitely something you want to look into.

Learn more at stripe.com

24. Gumroad

I actually just learned about Gumroad while writing this book. I was speaking to a client and business associate about pre-selling the book and she told me about it. I'm glad she did, because before I knew about it, I was only doing person-to-person sales having to exchange payment information from each person I spoke to instead of being able to share a link and make a sale. The first day I created an account, I made a pre-sale to someone I couldn't even recall ever seeing or speaking to just from posting the link on social media. It even offers a way to sell digital downloads and charge on a recurring basis. In addition to payment processing, Gumroad has a CRM solution as well, so you can better manage the relationship with the people who buy from you. Gumroad is definitely showing to be one of those must-haves in your list of payment options.

Learn more at Gumroad.com

25. Quickbooks

Having been around for many years, QuickBooks is still arguably the most popular accounting software for businesses with employees. Whereas other payment processing solutions focus mostly on the payment collection aspect of operating a business, QuickBooks gets more in depth with bookkeeping. It even has a platform specially designed for those classified as self-employed. What was once a software that had to be downloaded to a computer, QuickBooks is now available as a Cloud Accounting website known as QuickBooks Online. If you have a business that requires a lot of driving, you can actually track your deductible mileage with QuickBooks. It's also a great way to categorize your expenses, so you know exactly where your money is going. It even gives you cash flow charts, so you can easily track your profits and losses. If you have a business with hired employees, QuickBooks also offers a payroll processing solution, whereas you can even set up your employees for direct deposit payments.

Learn more at quickbooks.intuit.com

26. Peymynt

I was super excited when I learned about Peymynt. Because not only does it offer accounting and payment processing, it's also black-owned! Peymynt allows you to link your bank account, which will then give you access to cash flow charts and help you get prepared for filing tax returns. Not only can you send invoices with Peymynt, you can also set up reminders just in case someone forgets to pay. If you have customers or clients who request receipts for their payments, Peymynt has a solution for that also.

Learn more at peymynt.com

27. By The Book Accounting

Based in Duluth, Georgia, this black-owned accounting firm takes pride in keeping small businesses in business by offering services such as tax preparation, virtual CFO services and QuickBooks training. Learn more at bythebookaccounting.com

28. Elite Tax Co Software

Based in Houston, TX, this black-owned business offers a tax preparation software that aids in preparing for all types of tax returns including Schedules A, C, E, F, K-1, Forms 2106/4835 and many more. They even offer electronic signature pads like the ones most banks use. Even more impressive, they also offer a scanner that you can use to scan your W-2 and K-1 Forms to import data for your tax return. Not only do they provide software for tax preparation, they also have training videos that you can watch to learn how to use it. Are you interested in becoming a professional Tax Preparer? Elite Tax Co even offers what they call "Tax School" for people who want to become certified with the IRS. So, if you're in the Tax Preparation business, this might be something you'll want to look into.

Learn more at elitetaxcosoftware.com

Chapter 4

Documentation, Legalization, Loans & Grants

One of the most important things about owning a business is actually owning a "business." Meaning that you have a business registered with the Secretary of State that recognizes you as an Owner. In many cases, you can't even get funding for your business without the proper documentation. In order to open a business account for your business, you will definitely need official documentation to do so. In this chapter I'm going to present you with different solutions for documentation, legalization, loans and grants, so that you don't miss out on potential financial opportunities.

29. LegalZoom

LegalZoom is arguably the most popular way to get documentation for a business without having to deal with all of the ins and outs that come with it. Legal Zoom offers business formation services for registering sole-proprietorships, LLCs, corporations, DBAs, and EINs. They also offer services for people who want to create wills and trusts or protect their intellectual property with trademarks, patents and copyrights. LegalZoom can even help you get in touch with an Attorney by scheduling a call or finding one in their online directory. So, if you're someone who needs any of the aforementioned documents, but don't know how to go about getting them, then LegalZoom could be a great option for you.

Learn more at legalzoom.com

30. Skysthelimit.org

Skysthelimit.org is a non-profit organization geared towards training and educating people who want to start a business. Not only do they give you insight on how to officially register your business with the state, they also give you step-by-step guidance on the many aspects of starting and operating a business. Consider it "Entrepreneur School", because they literally train people on just about everything you will need to consider in order to create and maintain a successful business. Including knowing the basics of business, creating a business plan, how to pitch a business idea to potential investors and identifying your customers and how to best service them. They can even connect you with a mentor, if that's something you're interested in.

Learn more at skysthelimit.org

31. Dubsado

Dubsado is a business management solution designed to cut out the busywork. Build relationships, schedule appointments, and create workflows to streamline your projects from start to finish. I added Dubsado to this list, because it offers a feature for creating contracts and forms custom branded to your business. But, that's not all it offers. In addition to that, Dubsado also has features for client management, invoicing, appointment scheduling and accounting. If your business is client-based, meaning you deal heavily with contracts, appointments, short-term projects and/or invoicing, then Dubsado is something you may want to look further into.

Learn more at dubsado.com

32. Divine Notary, LLC

Divine Notary, LLC is a black-owned Notary Public business that aids people in legalizing documents such as contract agreements. Divine Notary offers an array of signing options for Refinancing, Loan Modifications, Vaccine Exemptions, Wills and Health Directives.

Learn more at divinenotaryllc.com

33. Small Business Administration

Created in 1953, the U.S. Small Business Administration (SBA) continues to help small business owners and entrepreneurs reach success. The SBA provides entrepreneurs and business owners with counseling, capital and contracting. So, basically they help you start a business, fund that business and even obtain government contracts. However, as I mentioned before, if you don't have the proper documentation, you could end up not qualifying for a loan or grant. Many of the loans and grants they offer are specific to people who are categorized in a specific group such as "minority" or "woman-owned" businesses. If you're planning to start a non-profit organization, staying up to date with what the SBA is offering could definitely benefit you.

Learn more at sba.gov

34. Google for Non-Profits

Adding to the many already available resources from Google, they now have solutions for non-profit organizations. If you plan on registering a non-profit organization and do a lot of advertising, Google now offers "Google Ad Grants", whereas your non-profit organization can be granted so much "money" in Google Ads per month. I actually just learned about this resource after seeing a post someone made with a screenshot of an email from Google letting them know that their non-profit organization had been granted $10,000 per month in Google Ads. They even offer their G-Suite to non-profits, so you can get a professional email and have access to many different applications for operating your business. To top it all off, Google for Nonprofits has a YouTube Program that makes it to where non-profit organizations can raise money through YouTube videos.

Learn more at google.com/nonprofits

35. WayFlyer

I actually just recently learned about this one. But, after researching it, it seems to be a great option for ecommerce businesses to get funding. But, not only does this site help businesses get funded, it also provides analytics for how well your marketing campaigns are doing. It actually integrates with Facebook Ads, Google Ads, Bing Ads and more.
Learn more at wayflyer.com

Chapter 5

Email Marketing & CRM

Even though social media has become the dominant way of marketing and communicating, email marketing still has its relevance and importance. Email marketing allows you to be more personable with your audience without having to directly speak to each person individually. By utilizing email marketing, you can keep track of who actually reads and engages with your emails, so that you can spend more time on maintaining a relationship with your most active audience. If you aren't already set on a service for email marketing and/or Customer Relationship Management, in this chapter, I'm going to give you a list of options.

36. Constant Contact

A pioneer in email marketing, Constant Contact is the email marketing solution for many large corporations. In addition to email marketing, Constant Contact now offers landing pages to sell products along with a website builder that comes equipped with eCommerce and Search Engine Optimization tools. Constant Contact integrates with Facebook, Instagram and Google Ads.. It even allows you to schedule posts to Facebook, Instagram and Twitter. Another cool aspect of this email marketing giant is that they now have Partner Programs, where you can resell their service to your clients. If you don't already have a website, a social media management service and/or you're looking for an all-inclusive email marketing solution, Constant Contact could very well be the one for you.

37. MailChimp

Another pioneer in email marketing, MailChimp still remains relevant in the business world. One of the most talked about features of MailChimp is that it's free for the first 1,000 subscribers. Like Constant Contact, MailChimp integrates with Facebook and Instagram ads as well. They also offer things like customizable forms and surveys to gather information and get feedback from your customers. In partnership with Square, MailChimp now offers what they call shoppable landing pages that come equipped with page analytics, where people can make purchases without you actually having a website.

Learn more at mailchimp.com

38. Flodesk

Flodesk is actually very new to me, so there isn't anything I can say about it from my own knowledge or experience, but based on what I've heard from other people and have seen in its presentation, I believe it's safe to say that when it comes to the overall look and feel of your emails, Flodesk definitely ranks among the top tools for email marketing. From what I've seen, it offers a large array of templates to enhance the presentation of your emails. According to a business associate of mine, Flodesk even has better automation than Mailchimp. Another thing I've noticed about Flodesk is its focus on optimizing how your emails look across different platforms. This way you can get a preview of what your emails will look like on desktops, tablets and mobile phones. If presentation is an important aspect for you when email marketing, then Flodesk could most definitely suffice as a viable option for you.

Learn more at flodesk.com

39. SalesForce

If you've worked in sales or customer service before, chances are you've at least heard about SalesForce even if you haven't actually used it. One of the greatest attributes I've noticed about SalesForce is the many different systems that it integrates with. While working in the health industry for Humana, Inc. as a Customer Service Specialist, I was introduced to the in-depth nature of it as I worked with a number of different platforms that worked hand-in-hand with the SalesForce platform. It's definitely one of the most, if not the most sophisticated, CRM platforms out there. SalesForce is so advanced, it would take a whole book in and of itself to cover everything about its features. If your business model is that of a rather complex one, whereas you have different departments within your business structure and a team of agents who help manage the relationships with those customers, then SalesForce would definitely meet your needs for customer relationship management.

Learn more at salesforce.com

40. Monday.com

Monday.com focuses the nature of its CRM platform on how easy it is to use. This tool was created for entrepreneurs, business owners and sales team leads who don't want to spend a lot of time setting up their CRM workflow, but would still like to use one that has an appealing look. It even has automation features that makes things like tracking sales leads and replying to emails seamless. If your business model relies heavily on a sales team and you'd prefer to utilize a CRM solution that makes it easy for you to get right to work without spending a lot of time setting things up, then Monday.com is what you may want to look further into.

Learn more at monday.com

41. Apptivo

I first learned about Apptivo while working on a sales team for a local radio station in Atlanta, Georgia. One of the greatest things I noticed about this platform is how advanced its integration features are. Apptivo integrates with many other popular platforms such as Dropbox, GSuite, Office365, PayPal, Slack and more. It also allows you to keep a good track of your contracts and invoices. In addition, it offers an email marketing solution as well. Based on the overall nature of its platform, I'd say anyone working in construction, real estate, home improvement and/or utility services, whereas your company deals a lot with contracts, various locations, work orders and estimates, then I would definitely suggest Apptivo to you.

Learn more at apptivo.com

42. Cloze Relationship Management

This mobile app based CRM platform is a newcomer to the world of customer relationship management. After researching what it has to offer, I would say it's most outstanding feature is how it automatically detects and identifies the social media pages of your contacts. Another great feature about it is how its algorithm is set up to identify your closest relationships with the people who matter to you the most. In addition, it's set up to make sure you never forget to follow-up with your contacts. In essence, this app serves as a Personal Assistant and Business Relationship Manager. If your business model relies a great deal on VIPs and you want to make sure you engage with them in the most efficient manner possible, then the Cloze Relationship Management App could very well be your go-to for a CRM solution.

Learn more at cloze.com

43. Thryv

Thryv is another CRM platform that I would say stands out because of its integration features. Thryv integrates with many other platforms such as Facebook, Instagram, Twitter, Wordpress, Square, PayPal, Quickbooks, Yelp and many more. It even has features for scheduling appointments, receiving reminders and sending text messages. Thryv also has a feature that gets you listed across 60+ listing sites. On top of all that, it has a way for you to store and share files with contacts. In comparison to other CRM solutions, Thyrv definitely ranks among the most all-inclusive platforms out there.

Learn more at thryv.com

Chapter 6

Directories & Listings

Okay, so, now you have a pretty well-oiled machine for a business model. You've taken care of important documents for your business. You've set up your social media accounts. You've purchased a web domain and you now have your website hosted online. You've even gathered an email list of contacts to keep in touch with via email marketing. But, what good is all that, if you have to always mention your brand in order to drive traffic and generate revenue. A great way to build awareness for your brand without having to be so active with promoting and marketing it is to have it listed in a business directory. So, in this chapter, I present to you some resources for listing your business online.

44. Google My Business

Chances are you've used Google to find a certain type of business that's in close proximity to your location. You may even use Google Maps to get driving directions to a business address. But, is your business listed in Google's network? Now, if you don't currently have a brick and mortar location for your business, then this doesn't serve you well, but if you do, then you should waste absolutely no more time getting listed. Getting listed is actually free and easy to do. All you need is a Google account. You can verify your business to get listed by either visiting at business.google.com or downloading the Google My Business mobile app.

Learn more at business.google.com

45. Yellow Pages

Having been around for more than 125 years, Yellow Pages is one of the oldest, if not the oldest, way to have a business listed for potential customers to find. Once referenced as a physical phone book, Yellow Pages now has an online directory. Just like with Google, having your business listed in the Yellow Pages is a free resource. So, if you have a physical business address that relies on foot traffic, why not take advantage of it?
Learn more at yellowpages.com

46. Yelp

A Yelp listing is another free one that you should definitely be taking advantage of, if you have a brick and mortar business location. Yelp is actually one of the more popular ways for people to find local businesses. Yelp makes it easy for potential customers to find local businesses based on the type of business they're looking for.

Learn more at yelp.com

47. Apple Maps

It's probably safe to say that more than half of people with mobile phones have iPhones. With that being said, having your business listed on Apple Maps is almost imperative and just like the aforementioned listings, it's free. So, if your business has a physical location, I wouldn't waste another second getting listed.

Learn more at <u>mapsconnect.apple.com</u>

48. WeBuyBlack

WeBuyBlack is arguably the most popular way to get sales online as a black-owned business outside of your own website. So, if you're someone who would be classified as "Black" or "African-American", this is something you definitely want to look into, if you haven't already. But, here's what makes WeBuyBlack so great. It's more than just a listing site...it's an online marketplace where black business owners from around the world can set up a store and sell products. With an online following of roughly one million, WeBuyBlack is hands down a great go-to for black-owned businesses that are product-based.

Learn more at <u>webuyblack.com</u>

49. Black Nation App

Black Nation App is another very popular resource for black-owned businesses. Not only does this app have a way for you to get your business listed in their directory, but their app is essentially a social networking platform like Facebook or Instagram. They even have a feature for businesses to do giveaways. If you're classified as a black business owner and your customer base or clientele mainly consists of so-called "Black" or "African-American" consumers and you want to be able to build and maintain a close relationship with them, then Black Nation App would definitely be your go-to.

Learn more at blacknation.app

50. Official Black Wall Street App

In my opinion, it's greatest feature is the one that notifies you when you're near a business listed in its directory. I have actually driven around in Atlanta, Georgia and received these notifications, which informed me about businesses I had never heard of. You can even pull up a map that will highlight black-owned businesses nearby you. This app also has a feature that allows you to promote your listing and show up at the top of the results when people search for businesses like yours. Does your business rely heavily on foot traffic? Are you considered a "Black" business owner? Then Official Black Wall Street App is definitely your go-to.

Learn more at officialblackwallstreet.com

51. Black Tradelines

This is another great resource for black-owned businesses to increase their exposure. Just like the Official Black Wall Street App, the Black Tradelines app makes it easy for you to find black-owned businesses within a close proximity. It's also set up like a social networking site where you can create a profile and interact with potential clients and customers. Even more impressive, Black TradeLines offers a way for you to get a business telephone number and up to 10 extensions that come with routing options. It even has a way for you to set up a live radio station and conference room. On top of all that, Black Trade Lines also offers loans to qualifying businesses. Out of all the black-owned business directory apps and websites, I would say that this one is definitely the most resourceful.

Chapter 7

Publications & Publishing Companies

In this chapter, I'm going to share with you some resources for educational reading materials and companies that can assist you in publishing a book. What good would this book be without references for other informative publications? So, of course I had to highlight the work of other coaches and consultants like myself. Maybe you have a great idea for a book, but need help publishing it? Well, this chapter is made specifically for you.

Publications

52. Entrepreneurs of Color Magazine

Entrepreneurs of Color Magazine is a business magazine that focuses its content around information about helpful tips, tools and resources to enhance the workflow of your business and balancing that with your everyday life. Entrepreneurs of Color Magazine also focuses on spotlighting so-called "Black" or "African-American" entrepreneurs who haven't yet been featured in mainstream media. So, chances are this could also be a resource for publicity.

Learn more at eocmagazine.biz

53. You Lost Me @ Hello

Recognized as "The Business Revenue Accelerator", the Author of this book, Donna Smith Bellinger, is undoubtedly a mastermind at making sales and increasing business revenue. She is actually my personal Sales Coach, who I can honestly say has helped me generate more cash flow with her ideas and insight. As stated in its description, this book provides the HOW and the WHY for creating memorable impressions and developing sustaining relationships in business and life.

Purchase this book at Amazon.com

54. 5 Tips for Entrepreneurs, Small Business Owners and Service Professionals to Survive COVID-19 and Beyond

Written by Arlicia Nixon, this ebook is a valuable guide for entrepreneurs, small business owners and service professionals on ways that they can sustain their businesses and clientele during a time of economic crisis affected by the Covid-19 pandemic. It is also resourceful, for those business owners, whether service or product based who are looking for practical solutions to resolving stagnancy and growing with the current economic climate and culture as to how they do business. It highlights the importance of accurately assessing the condition of your business, winning clients, business ethics during a crisis, the importance of establishing products and services that are needs based, and continuing to learn and grow as a small business owner or entrepreneur.

Purchase this book at gumroad.com/l/ZWSeg

55. Are You Sure That You Are Ready?: A Guide for Vendors

If you are currently a business owner or you're considering becoming one that intends to use Vending and Craft events as an option to increase sales and exposure, THIS is the book to read! Ms E is sharing her knowledge and expertise based on being in business for over 12 years, having gone to events in and outside of the city of Cleveland, while building relationships in the process, so that you will yield results without it costing you the hefty price of "trial & error" on your own.

Purchase this book at Amazon.com

56. The Misadventures of a New Entrepreneur: 5 Things They Won't Teach You in Business School

So, you want to be an entrepreneur? There's bad news and good news.
Entrepreneur and business consultant, Andrena Sawyer, shares the secrets that every new entrepreneur should know. From the value of infrastructure to remaining relevant, aspiring and operational entrepreneurs will learn.

Purchase this book at Amazon.com

57. Build a Legit Business

Written by Chayla Jackson, this book is written for today's entrepreneur navigating business and all that comes with it especially in the age of COVID-19. One thing remains the same and that is the laws of doing business. They do not disappear and an entrepreneur's ignorance of the law can cost them a pretty penny and shatter their dreams before they get the business off the ground or shut it down after they've worked so hard to build the brand, generate good relationships with customers and clients, and turn a profit.

This book will give you the legal knowledge to equip you to use the law to build and protect your business, brand and wealth.

Purchase this book at iamchylajackson.thrivecart.com

58. A Black Butterfly's Journey Towards CLAR.R.R.ITY: Reveal Renew Reignite!

A Black Butterfly's Journey Towards CLAR.R.R.ITY: Reveal Renew Reignite! is a book to give you clarity in realizing your God-given potential and purpose. A heartwarming conversation puts to rest old narratives in a way that honors your journey, thus promoting new thinking and new ways of being. As a result, the "CLAR.R.R.ITY" that allows you to honor yourself, your family, community, and Creator are renewed.

Purchase this book at Amazon.com

59. Why You SUCK at Network Marketing

President and CEO of Building Bridges Consulting, Coach Niquenya D. Fulbright, explains exactly why the average network marketer completely fails at multi-level marketing opportunities. Coach Niquenya provides an overview of the top 4 critical mistakes that network marketers make to S.U.C.K. so badly at making any profits. She also shares a proven process she uses and teaches to her entrepreneur clients to ensure their success. This book is for network marketers, multi-level marketing teams, sales people, and any entrepreneur seeking to catapult their long-term business success by following a scalable, sustainable, and profitable business model.

Purchase this book at Amazon.com

Publishing Companies

60. JNF Enterprises

This Baltimore-based black-owned business is actually the editor of this book. So, if you've enjoyed reading so far, that is partly because of their services. The President Leroy Mckenzie, Jr., has written a number of books himself as well as been featured as a keynote speaker in numerous arenas. His knowledge of the industry continues to evolve, even though he's seasoned as a businessman.

Learn more at jnfenterprises.com

61. Perfect Time SHP, LLC Coaching, Consulting, and Book Publishing Firm

Perfect Time SHP, LLC Coaching, Consulting, and Book Publishing Firm offers a ONE STOP SHOP for the author who is looking to get published. With a team of professional coaches and consultants, Perfect Time SHP is no doubt a package deal. Established in 2017, Perfect Time SHP LLC Book Publishing is the result of the desire to alleviate barriers to aspiring authors getting their book published.

Learn more at getpublishedwithdrsharon.com

62. SMS Write On Publishing, LLC

This black-owned, New York based publishing company was founded by Shannon Spruill. Shannon graduated Suma Cum Laude from Bryant and Stratton College with a bachelor's degree in Business Administration and a master's degree in Biblical Studies. As an Author of numerous books herself, Shannon is definitely well-versed in the publishing industry having published her first book on December 1st, 2010.

Learn more at smswriteonpub.com

63. Life Bridge Publishing

The Founder of this black-owned publishing company is Ashley Graham, an Author, Poet and Business Coach. Authors may experience several hurdles in their journey to be published. Ashley Graham experienced this struggle firsthand and launched Lift Bridge so the lifetime achievement of getting published could be an enjoyable chapter in authors' stories everywhere. She also has a podcast titled, "Finish Your Book Already" stemming from a strategy session designed to coach Authors in the writing process.

Learn more at lbpub.com

64. Written Words Publishing LLC

Located in Aurora, Colorado, this black-owned publishing company is actually accredited by the Better Business Bureau. They offer 10% off self-publishing and editing services for new customers. Having satisfied countless customers in the past, this company could be a great option for anyone looking to publish a book or have it edited.
Learn more at writtenwordspublishing.com

65. OFFprint Publishing

OFFprint Publishing is another great publishing company to consider working with. They focus their niche on working especially with Black Authors and turning their written books into audiobooks. They even have a page on their website dedicated to spotlighting featured Authors who they've worked with. The CEO, Stephanie Michele, is a professional musician, singer, songwriter, filmmaker, sound engineer, educator and producer who has pulled skills from all of those experiences and funneled them into the OFFprint brand.

Learn more at offprintpublishing.com

Chapter 8

Audio & Video Production & Broadcasting

With the rise in technology comes the continued increase in how much technology is used by businesses to attract and retain customers and clients. If you're not using some form of audio or video production and/or broadcasting, then you're going to limit your market share. So, in this chapter, I'm going to share with you some solutions for producing and broadcasting audio and video.

66. YouTube

I'm sure you've at least heard of YouTube. But, the question is, "Are you utilizing it?" and if so, are you maximizing your results by taking advantage of its various ways to gain exposure on its platform? Well, even if you're not many companies are. In fact, it's talked about that many companies of all sizes are spending less money advertising on Facebook and more on YouTube. If you gain a large enough audience, you can actually get paid for having ads shown on your channel. If you're looking to run an ad yourself, you can actually utilize Google's Display Network to specifically target YouTube videos that attract people with similar interests to those of your target audience. Want to broadcast live? You can do so with Google Hangouts and it will not only broadcast your video live on a YouTube link, but it will also save the video to your channel after it's finished.

Learn more at YouTube.com

67. Zoom

Zoom has become one of the most popular ways, if not the most popular way to host meetings, conferences, webinars, classes and video broadcasts. With Zoom you can host private meetings with clients and/or your team or you can publicly broadcast live shows. There's even a way for you to record video and download it to your PC.

Learn more at zoom.us

68. Anchor

Anchor is arguably the best way to create and distribute a podcast. With many different easy-to-use creation tools, Anchor gives you the power to record audio on various platforms, build episodes, import audio or video and add background music. Not to mention it offers free hosting and distribution. With Anchor you can distribute your podcasts to many other popular podcast platforms such as Spotify, Apple and Google. It also comes equipped with analytics, so that you can take a closer look at where most of your listeners are coming from.

Learn more at anchor.fm

69. Apple Garageband

If you have an iPhone, iPad or Mac computer, then you have access to this audio recording and engineering software. Why pay so much for an Apple device, if you're not going to utilize as many of its features as possible? With Garageband, you can record songs and audio commercials that can be uploaded to your podcast or used to distribute to advertising platforms.

Learn more at apple.com/mac/garageband

70. Audacity

Even if you don't have an Apple device, you can still take advantage of a free software for audio recording and engineering. For years, Audacity has been a go-to option for people looking to record audio. With free tools like Garageband and Audacity, there's no excuse for why you don't have an audio commercial for your brand.

Learn more at audacityteam.org

71. Blog Talk Radio
I first learned about Blog Talk Radio in 2011 while networking with other Spoken Word Artists like myself. Blog Talk Radio is a great way to host a radio show that people can easily listen to by simply calling in from their phone. The dashboard has ways for you to input audio in case you want to play music and/or run ads on your radio show. Blog Talk Radio has many different categories that people can browse through, making it easy for you to reach your target audience.
Learn more at blogtalkradio.com

72. Ripl

I first learned about Ripl back in 2016 while looking for a way to produce video ads. At that time, it was rather new on the scene and its platform was completely free. Since then, Ripl has grown its popularity by implementing many new features including 1000s of templates, stock photos and videos, over 150 fonts, 100s of music tracks, and social sharing, where you can easily share your videos to social media and track the results. Even though it's no longer free, you can take advantage of a 7-day free trial.

Learn more at ripl.com

Podcasts

73. Bshani Radio App

Founded by Bennie Randall Jr., this black-owned radio app has become a very reliable resource for many entrepreneurs, business owners and content creators. Not only does it feature podcasts that include valuable information for how to better operate and structure your business, but it also provides a way for you to create a podcast show of your own. The great thing about it is it doesn't take up much memory space on your phone. The Bshani Radio Network is three years old with over 2,000 episodes broadcasting to listeners in the United States, Zimbabwe, Germany, Canada and the United Kingdom. With over 2 million downloads, the Bshani Radio App is an excellent way to learn and build exposure for your brand.

74. Conversations with Chan

Created by Chandra Gore, "Conversations with Chan" is a podcast that focuses its content on entrepreneurship, business tips and more. With featured guests who are seasoned as entrepreneurs, this podcast is a great way to learn more about how to be successful as an entrepreneur.

Learn more at anchor.fm/conversationswithchan

75. The CEO Launch

Hosted by Bernadette L. Harris and Kenya L. Johnson, The CEO Launch is a weekly discussion exploring the good, bad and ugly of early entrepreneurship. More than just tips and tricks, this mother-daughter duo sheds light on the humanness of being a business owner by giving you deep, honest, and sometimes comedic conversations about their entrepreneurial journey.

Learn more at theceolaunch.com

76. The Convo with Kisha

"The Convo with Kisha" highlights some of the most intriguing and fascinating people in the world. From Money Whisperers to Career coaches, there are dozens of convos that will help you either in business or life.

Learn more at convowithkisha.com

77. The Collaborative Culture

The Collaborative Culture podcast focuses on building collaborative communities through knowledge, interviews & shared experiences in business. Collaboration is more than just putting a group of people together, it's about creating the right workflow of people & processes to create that magic that makes your brands unique. We are committed to helping you build collaborative cultures & becoming a strategic collaborator! Join your host Ali Joseph as she discusses the power in meaningful partnerships to scale!

78. Pep Talk with Tisha Hammond

"Pep Talk with Tisha Hammond"...Powered by Dell Technologies and Intel' is a show that discusses the growing joys and pains of entrepreneurship while celebrating the wins of every size for the Guest Star. It's an extensive video library that celebrates entrepreneurship and spotlights those who call themselves "Boss."

Listen at YouTube.com

Chapter 9

Cloud Storage and Team Communications

These days because social media and online marketing and networking have basically become the centerpiece of how most businesses operate, having a way to store and organize media files is just as important. Furthermore, if you are working with a team of people, you need a way to collectively share and review digital files to make for effective collaboration. So, in this chapter I will share with you solutions for storing digital files in an online cloud storage and communicating effectively as a team.

Cloud Storage

79. Google Drive

Adding to the many business solutions that Google offers, Google Drive is arguably the most popular resource for cloud storage. With Google Drive, you can not only store but create files such as word documents, spreadsheets, slideshow presentations and more. There are many other popular platforms that integrate with Google Drive to upload files. You can also create a sharable link to publicly display your creations in addition to giving other people access to edit or comment.

Learn more at drive.google.com

80. OneDrive

OneDrive is Microsoft's approach to an online cloud storage solution. If you often use platforms from Microsoft such as Outlook, Word, Excel and/or PowerPoint then OneDrive makes it easy for you to store and organize those files online, so you don't run the risk of losing access to them in the event that your PC breaks down.

Learn more at office.live.com

81. DropBox

DropBox is another cloud storage solution that many people use which has been around for a while. But, there's "DropBox" and then there's "DropBox Business." With DropBox Business you can integrate with Google Docs, Sheets, and Slides, Microsoft Office files, Slack, Trello and Zoom.

Learn more at dropbox.com/business

Team Communications

82. Slack

After being introduced to Slack by Incluzion, a recruiting and job search solution, which I will mention later in this book, I would say that Slack is very sophisticated, because its interface allows you to create threads as a way to filter conversations and subject matters. Slack is integratable with over 2,000 other popular platforms such as Google's G-Suite, Zoom, DropBox, Microsoft OneDrive, and monday.com.

Learn more at slack.com

83. Trello

Trello is constantly growing in popularity when it comes to project management and team organization. Trello helps you keep track of what you're working on, what you've completed and what you've delegated. Trello integrates with other platforms such as Google Drive, DropBox, Slack and more. If you deal with due dates regularly, Trello is a great tool for keeping track of them.

Learn more at trello.com

84. Microsoft Teams

I was first introduced to Microsoft Teams while working as a Customer Service Agent for Humana, Inc. With Microsoft Teams, you can send instant messages, make voice and video calls, schedule meetings and more. You can also create chat rooms designated for specific teams or departments, making team communication very easy to manage and keep track of. Microsoft Teams is integratable with over 500 other platforms such as Skype, MailChimp, YouTube and Adobe Creative Cloud.

85. Goals App

With Goals App, you can create competitions and set goals for your team and reward them for reaching those goals. It comes with a customizable point system that allows your team members to keep track of their progress. You can even create prizes for team members to redeem their points. Whether it is paid time off, a physical gift or a vacation voucher. Goals App allows you to create an environment that will keep your team motivated and their morale high.

Learn more at goals.app

86. Airtable

Airtable is a great tool for organizing many different things. It can be used to manage inventory, projects and leads, list contacts, strategize marketing campaigns and much more. You can even use it to streamline your interviewing process in the event that you're looking to hire employees or contractors. If you're in the Human Resources industry or have HR as a part of your business model, then Airtable is definitely a great tool for you to consider.

Learn more at Airtable.com

Chapter 10

Coaches & Consultants

One of the greatest resources you can have as an entrepreneur and business owner is an insightful coach or consultant. I'm sure you've heard the idiom "It's not what you know. It's who you know." I personally feel as if that statement is just as valid today as it was when it was first coined and will continue to be valid, as valuable relationships with key people will always be a pathway to success. Even if you are a coach or consultant yourself, it's still in your best interest to have those other more experienced coaches and consultants in your network. With all that being said, in this chapter, I will share with you some of the leaders who I personally look up to.

87. Tajuana Ross

Internationally recognized as "The LinkedIn Professor" and affectionately known as My Coach Tajuana, Tajuana Ross has graced the stages of many different platforms and enhanced the brands of countless clients making her an award winning speaker. Not only has she established herself as a bestselling author, every client she has worked with has also been recognized as such. Her clientele base is outstanding and the results of working with her are undeniable. One thing about Tajuana is she is serious about success and if you want to work with her, you have to be just as serious.

Learn more at workwithtajuana.com

88. Dr. Cozette M. White

Dealing with the IRS can be very stressful. Thankfully, we have Dr. Cozette M. White as a resource for counseling on how to deal with the IRS. Dr. White has helped thousands scale their businesses by maximizing revenue, managing cash flow and creating tax shelters.

Learn more at myfinancialhome.com

89. Sophia Casey

Life and Leadership Coach, Sophia Casey, is an international award winning speaker, corporate trainer, author and executive coach. She serves as an instructor for personal and professional development coaches. She enjoys empowering people to live fully with leadership, ownership and accountability.

Learn more at easeandflowacademy.thinkific.com

90. Zhe L. Scott

After reading this far into the book, if you don't already know, you would come to the conclusion that having a significant web presence is imperative to the success of your business. Thankfully, we have Zhe L. Scott to school us in building a web presence and having a website show up in Google Search results. Internationally known as "The SEO Queen", Zhe specializes in search engine optimization and overall website performance. She has a variety of tools on her website that you can use to validate your website's SEO performance. She actually gets over 400 searches on Google per year of her name alone. She's gotten over 300 websites listed on page 1 of Google Search results and has generated over $60 million in revenue for all of her clients combined.

Learn more at www.theseoqueen.net

91. WendyY Bailey

For nearly 20 years, WendyY has helped hundreds of clients build and scale their business, accelerate their income and grow their bottom line profits. Focusing her niche on helping clients find the confidence in their sales voice, WendyY has established herself as an expert and mastermind in the sales industry. She is recognized as a genius on sales strategies and conversations that convert into profit. Having reached so many milestones in her work, WendyY is recognized as a Coach among Coaches.

Learn more at businessbeyondlimits.com

93. Arian Hargrove

Recognized as "Your Systems Queen", Arian Hargrove is an expert at streamlining processes, workflows and day-to-day operations. She helps entrepreneurs, small businesses and large corporations alike with implementing systems that will make for a highly efficient workflow as it pertains to team building and communications. A one-on-one session with Arian will give you in-depth insight on how to set up and organize your business operations, so that you and your team have a clear understanding of respective roles and responsibilities.

Learn more at love4systems.com

94. Bro Bedford

Bro. Bedford specializes in helping Black people discover their entrepreneurial and business greatness. He's been seen and heard on NBC, CBS, Radio One, iHeart Radio and numerous other radio shows, television programs, podcasts and websites around the world. He has addressed audiences as large as 20,000 sharing the stage with entertainers, sports stars, celebrities and legendary entrepreneurs and thought leaders such as George Fraser, Les Brown, Dr. Dennis Kimbro, Susan Taylor, Lisa Nichols and Julianne Malveaux just to name a few.

Learn more at brobedford.com

95. Amari Asad

Amari Asad is Founder & President of Amari's Mentoring Program. Amari's mentoring provides life coaching, business management & mentoring programs for Individuals and organizations alike. Amari is a graduate of Dowling College in Oakdale New York, where he received a BA in Business Management and a BA in Social Work with a minor in Education. Amari understands that "Knowledge of self is the key to your success in life." This way of thinking has led to

Mr. Asad having become who he is today, a world-renowned Motivational Speaker and the author of the book entitled "Empowered: Insights of Amari Asad."

Learn more at www.amariasad.org

Chapter 11

Public Relations & Recruiting

In addition to administration, marketing and sales, public relations is another very important element to success in business. In my opinion, because publicity is, in essence, someone else advocating for you, it is undoubtedly the best way to gain exposure for a brand. Not only because you get a chance to present to a potentially larger audience, but because it allows you to be specific with your targeting, tell your story and give updates about your business. Along with publicity, as your business continues to grow, recruiting reliable candidates will become more and more important. In this last chapter, I will share with you some resources for gaining publicity and recruiting potential candidates.

Public Relations

96. BlackPR.com

BlackPR.com is arguably the most inexpensive and highly effective way to gain publicity for a brand targeted towards those identified as "Black." I have personally used it as a public relations resource myself and in doing so, generated more exposure for my brand than I was used to. I even had to hire an Assistant to help me keep up with all of the new emails and inquiries that were coming in as a result of distributing a press release with blackpr.com. With an email list of over 30,000 black-owned media outlets including BET, Oprah Winfrey Network and TV One and a social media network of about 1 million or more, BlackPR..com is undoubtedly a reliable resource for going public.

Learn more at blackpr.com

97. Pam Perry

Pam Perry is an award-winning communications professional and publisher of Speakers Magazine. She teaches and mentors authors, speakers and entrepreneurs on how to build a platform and attract major media attention and clients. After working with Pam, her clients have been featured on CNN, TBN, The Word Network, Radio One, Oprah Magazine, Tom Joyner Morning Show, Essence, Ebony, Black Enterprise, PBS and many other major media outlets. Her clients have been offered major publishing contracts, created successful full-time careers and "Authorpreneurs" earning six-figures.

Learn more at pamperrypr.com

98. Lemon-Lime Light Media

Founded by La'Torria Lemon in 2011, Lemon-Lime Light Media is a full service Public Relations, Branding, Consulting, Marketing and Event activation firm based in Houston and Atlanta. With almost 10 years in the industry, Lemon-Lime Light Media and team have accomplished a plethora of achievements and campaigns for notable clients and brands such as BET, TNT, VH1, Oprah Winfrey Network, Radio-One and countless others. Having been recognized as one of the top 50 entrepreneurs in Texas, La'Torria Lemon is undoubtedly one of the best in the industry.

Learn more at lemonlimelightmedia.com

Recruiting

99. Black Virtual Assistants

Black Virtual Assistants was founded on the principles of community, support, education, networking and fundamental training for new and existing Black (African-American) Virtual Assistants. In addition to a directory of Black VAs and a magazine about the virtual assistant industry, Black Virtual Assistants also offers a membership program for anyone looking to learn more about being a successful Virtual Assistant. The Black Virtual Assistants Magazine is a publication that showcases the bios and photos of professional black virtual assistants. It features tools, resources, tips and profound advice for those seeking virtual assistant services or a career in virtual assisting.

Learn more at blackvirtualassistants.com

100. Incluzion

Incluzions Founder, Jibril Sulaiman, is an entrepreneur of 20 years and has an innate passion to provide economic empowerment for marginalized communities. In 2019, his passion led him to launch Incluzion - a community of

Women, Black and Latinx professionals working in a flexible capacity (remote professionals, freelancers and consultants).

As the Founder and CEO of Incluzion, Jibril leads a team whose mission is to provide Black and Latinx talent with the resources and support that they need to thrive as remote, freelance or work-from-home professionals.

Learn more at incluzion.com

About the Author

WHO IS PREECH?

Born in Pensacola, Florida and given the name Jordan Nichols at birth, this young entrepreneur has already established himself as a Subject Matter Expert and is now recognized as a Marketing and Branding Consultant. You may know him by his spiritual name, Yerodin Ghedi Adwin Beluchi or by his stage name, Preech.

After making a name for himself as a Spoken Word Artist in the South, he founded Black History Enterprises LLC while living in Atlanta, Georgia in 2017. His inspiration was to preserve and highlight the struggles and accomplishments of people of African descent while serving the greater community. Since officially taking on the life of an entrepreneur at the age of 20, Preech has found his niche as a writer, performer and event organizer. He is most respected and regarded for his work as the Editor-in-chief of Entrepreneurs of Color Magazine.

WHAT'S HIS MOTIVATION?

"I have had the honor of reading the works and witnessing the teachings of those who many refer to as Master Teachers. So-called "African-American" men and women who have established themselves as scholars and influential leaders...these elders and ancestors that I'm referring to have dedicated their lives to the study and teaching of their scholastic discoveries; many of which were not widely taught. Through their efforts, they enlightened and educated me and many others on the unfortunate struggles and great accomplishments of people of African descent and therefore have encouraged and motivated me to dedicate myself to this great cause in my own unique and creative way."

Preech

Learn more at bookwithpreech.com